DATE DUE

Celso

Leo Romero

Arte Público Press
Houston
1985

appeared in the follow-
Puerto Del Sol, Foot-
v, San Marcos Review,
rfano, La Confluencia
Magazine, Santa Fe Poetry Review, Grito Del Sol, The Indian Rio Grande (an anthology by San Marcos Press), and a chapbook, *During The Growing Season* (Maguey Press, 1978). I wish to thank the National Endowment for the Arts for a fellowship which allowed me the time to complete this manuscript.

L.R.

Cover design by Narciso Peña.

Arte Público Press
University of Houston
University Park
Houston, Texas 77004

CONTENTS

CELSO'S ADOPTIVE MOTHER (I)

THE MIRACLE (II)

ESTRELLITA'S LIPS (III)

THE GOSPEL ACCORDING TO CELSO (IV)

A LOST SOUL (V)

BREATH OF FLOWERS (VI)

This book is dedicated to those who see a little bit of Celso in themselves.

CELSO'S ADOPTIVE MOTHER (I)

Celso's Adoptive Mother

Celso's mother died shortly
after giving birth
and his father disappeared
without a trace

He was brought up
by María, his mother's
oldest sister

Blessed was María
among all women
She was never married
and yet she had Celso as a son

Celso's Father

When he was a child
Celso was always being asked
who his father was

He died in the war
Celso would answer curtly

The war, people would say
with a questioning tone
Which war

The one in which he died
Celso would respond
and then turn about abruptly
and flee from their next question

People never let up
They hounded him about the matter
The only solution was to run

When other children
asked him who his father was
he found it easier
to continue the lie

His father had died in the war
It had been the last war
His father had been blown up
So there wasn't a grave

Celso avoided adults
like the plague

He never went into

his friends' houses
Their parents' first question
never varied

But when Celso became a man
and people would ask him
who his father had been
He would answer them bluntly
that he was the product
of an immaculate conception
just like Jesus
but that he had no great plans
for the salvation of mankind

And damn if he'd die
on a cross
for their sins

A Pillow Full of Feathers

As a child Celso did many cruel things
like tossing a gunnysack
full of kittens to the pigs
and even once he grabbed
a chicken by the neck
and tried to whirl it over his head
like he had seen men do
when killing chickens

One day he discovered
that if he stood under a magpie's nest
and whistled loudly
the young birds would grow panic-stricken
with wings too weak to fly

But the worst thing he ever did
was when he came across two owls
in an arroyo in daylight
and mercilessly threw rocks at them

Then one day after a rain
he came across a sick mouse
which shivered helplessly
and didn't attempt to run away
Celso built a circular wall of rock
around the mouse
intending to topple it on the tiny creature
but once the wall was built
he grew frightened
and finally ran away crying

After that Celso prayed many rosaries
and he went to confession
For penance the priest told him

to climb a hill with a pillow full of feathers
and to scatter them in the wind
and all these he was to collect
Celso sighed with relief
for supposedly a woman in the village
had been told to pick up grains of salt
with her eyelashes

The Rooster

I was a young boy
when the rooster
had his head cut off
Celso started his story

But do you know
that rooster wouldn't die
It seemed as if the sky
was awash with blood

The headless rooster chased
me around the plum tree
like a frisky goat
I nearly screamed

I half expected the rooster
to peck me with his sharp beak
I could still see his red comb
but it was the blood pouring

We ate the rooster
that same day
and I remember its meat
tasted a little tough

I never saw the rooster
stop jumping around
Last time I looked back
it was still after me

Somehow it died
but I didn't watch
One skinny, tough rooster
which had made the chickens fly

Where do eggs come from
I whispered
and my aunt grew red
Eat, she said

And we bowed our heads
in prayer
for this skinny rooster
which didn't taste too good

The Moon and Angels

I remember once as a child
traveling at night
and watching the moon
It is following me, I thought
It is my own guardian angel
like the one pictured
in the catechism books

All holy things glow
The stars, the sun
the moon and angels
Celso, I thought to myself
you are someone special
What have you done to make
the moon follow you like a dog

And I remembered that
I had been to confession that day
and when I walked out of the church
the world was different
clearer, a little like heaven

When I had walked into the church
my heart had felt
like a dirty, ragged bag
filled with drowned kittens
But when I walked out the door
my heart was buoyant
afloat in the air
higher than any bird

That must be it, Celso
I thought
The moon is attracted

to the pure silver
of your heart
untarnished by sin

And I reasoned that the moon
was the halo of an angel
looking down from heaven
and thus could be seen
the top of his head

THE MIRACLE (II)

The Miracle

Celso had a vision
He saw the face of Jesus
on the wall of a small house
by the church in Agua Negra
He would pass by there each night
on his way home from the bar
usually so drunk on wine
that he would see two of everything
And in fact he saw two Jesuses
though he knew there was but one

By next day everyone had heard
of Celso's vision
That night there were hundreds of people
from the many mountain villages
gathered to see the miracle
Some said they saw the face of Jesus
others saw Satan, Mary, a Lamb
a Cross, and one little girl
even claimed to see the Last Supper
Those who saw nothing were quiet

Holy Water

For Easter, Celso put a sign
by the river reading
HOLY WATER — 50 CENTS A BUCKET FULL
People were suspicious at first
How can you make such a claim
they would say
eyeing the river doubtfully

I had the priest bless the river
Celso would say
And now and forever
the flowing water of this river
will be holy water
but only between these two stakes
And Celso would point to two sticks
twenty yards apart

That is only as far
as the priest walked
before he fell into the river
and drowned thus becoming a saint
It is only while the water
is between these two stakes
that it is holy

Celso's Dream

Procopio, last night
I had a dream
in which the air
was filled
with skeletal angels

they swarmed
like millions of moths
obscuring the sun

And when they came
to the earth
they sank
into the ground
into their graves

Leaving
only their wings
which rose
into the air

And it was then,
Procopio, that I heard
the heavenly
songbirds sing
this song

Farewell
to your earthly cages
The earth is welcome
to your bones
But heaven-bound
are your wings

Across Pitch Black Forests and Meadows

Listen to Celso

My friend's wife
shot herself
She was pregnant

My friend told me
that he walked
straight into the mountains
tirelessly
and didn't stop
until it was night
He slept for a while
and dreamt about birds

He woke abruptly
and was amazed to see
the sky thickly covered
with the eyeballs
of the dead
They were chirping
to each other
across pitch black
forests and meadows

Celso is spreading
the rumor
that death
is a blossoming
And that the heart
opens its mouth
like a red rose

Roses Blooming in the Snow

It rained hard all day, after the rain
Celso went outside and found
the chicken house missing
The river had carried it away
Celso ran after the river
screaming at the top of his lungs
He ran along the swollen river bank
and found one chicken in the mud

Celso cursed and shook his fists at the sky
He hurried to the church in Agua Negra
and looked accusingly at the saints
When he was sure no one else was in the church
Celso turned the saints so they faced the wall
This will teach you, Celso grumbled

Next day everyone in Agua Negra marveled
that the statues of the saints had moved
And the priest declared to his congregation
that there couldn't have been any greater miracle
even if they had heard bells ringing in the earth
or seen roses blooming in the snow

Angel Hair

Celso keeps three long strands
of white angel hair
in a metal box
When he gets drunk
he shows it to people
but tells them not to touch
or they will burn their hands

Where did you find this hair
people ask him
I woke up one night he says
and caught my guardian angel napping
I pulled his hair to teach him
to be more vigilant
And that is how I came to have
this withered hand

Lake of Sorrow

I had been drinking all day
Celso began his story
When I left the bar
I couldn't tell
which way was up
and which way was down
much less which way
to head home
Next thing I remember
was waking up in the mountains
half frozen to death

Celso waits for someone
to refill his glass
before continuing his story

The sun was just rising
above the mountains
so I began walking
to bring warmth
to my chilled body
I soon came across
a small stream
of clear blue water
I drank my fill
and then I heard
a bittersweet music
that made my heart weep

I followed the stream
until I reached a lake
At first the water
was very still
but suddenly

it grew agitated
and a woman rose
out of the middle of the lake

A murmur passed
through the crowd of men
who had gathered
to hear Celso's story
Celso paused to have
his empty glass refilled
but that was not
the only reason
why he had paused
Celso was making up
the story
as he was telling it
and he was stuck

After a few minutes
the crowd began
to press Celso
Tell us more, Celso
someone yelled
Was it the Virgin Mary
a timid voice asked
Tell us what she said
several voices spoke at once

Yes, the woman I saw
was the Virgin Mary
Celso said with authority
He then lowered his head
as if in prayer
Everyone else did the same
After a minute of thinking hard
Celso came up with an idea

The Virgin Mary has taken
a personal interest
in your lives
For months she has kept
a close watch on you
day and night
The men grew fidgety

You have caused her
great sorrow
Celso said
pointing around the room
at random

Her message is
that your sinful lives
have filled her heart
with sorrow
And this sorrow
has overflowed
and formed a lake
around her
She weeps for your
immortal souls
day and night

Slowly one by one
the men put down
their glasses of wine
and each headed home
without uttering a word
Lost in their own thoughts

Looking around the empty bar
Celso sighed with relief
But then thinking

of what he had said
he began to believe
his own words
and he too headed home
Probing his heart and soul

ESTRELLITA'S LIPS (III)

Estrellita's Lips

Celso kissed Estrellita's lips
and they reminded him of wine
I get drunk every time I kiss her
Celso would explain
to anyone who would ask if he was in love

Like cheap wine her lips
don't cost much
but they go straight to the head

The heart, the heart
people would say
that is what matters, not the head

But Celso was adamant
the head is the house of the soul
the heart is a flea-bitten bed
a restless night, a terrible complaint
Only the head, the head
adding, subtracting
multiplying, such is love

Una Canción de Flores

Listen to Celso
and you'd think anything was possible

Celso claims the moon is a woman
who carries a large knife
He has seen her cut down stars
which came too close

> Anoche la luna
> salió de los árboles
> con un cuchillo largo

> La luna tiene cabello blanco
> ojos blancos
> labios blancos

Celso has heard the moon sing
songs of flowers

Celso carries a long knife
to be like the moon
He tells everyone he is in love
and brandishes the knife gently
as if he were beheading roses

Celso, Moonstruck

Fideligna, do you know
what it is like to be in love
with a sphere, an apparition
a luminous glow
Here where the heart should be
there is a hole
deep and straight as a well
where there is nothing but darkness

Fideligna, do you know
what it is like
not to be able to sleep at night
To prowl like a cat
with eyes that reflect
the brightness of that orb
that face hinting a thousand other faces
How can I sleep when my head
is crammed with a thousand shapes
a thousand thoughts
all about the same thing

And all the time there is this hole
through which stars could fit
this yearning
Fideligna, am I crazy
to be so much in love
that I have lost my heart
To be so much in love with a ghost
a spirit that glides
through the night sky
indifferent, singing a song
that afflicts me
and which I never understand

Fideligna, I fear

that if I could grab
hold of this love
it would turn to ice
And that there is nothing
nothing that could ever
fill this emptiness
that displaced my heart

Dancing with Moonlight

I have not told you, have I
of the night I danced with moonlight
Celso says sitting back in the chair
and stroking the stubble on his chin

I have not told anyone before, Celso says
because then people would have had
just cause to call me crazy
Not just because I danced with moonlight
but because I fell in love
And with what — moonbeams, shimmering light
Nothing anyone can get a firm hold of

I can still remember how softly
the moonlight pressed against my chest
I cannot remember when I enjoyed
dancing so much
It was as if we were not touching earth
We glided through the night as one heart
And when the moon lifted her head
I kissed those lips
which were as white as snow
But there was no coldness to them
they were sweet tasting and warm

It was only one night, says Celso
but since then I have danced
with moonlight in my mind
I can now understand my aunt's madness
When I was a child I peeked into her room
the room was filled with moonlight
and she was dancing naked
before the open window

When moonlight gets into your brain
it is called madness
but when it gets into your heart
it is called love, says Celso
His thoughts drifting away
to that one night he danced with moonlight

Love Makes Fools of Us All

Because the moon is a woman
I love the moon, says Celso
You see how far away the moon is
There is a reason, he explains
to anyone who asks if he has ever loved
one woman more than any other

I loved her so much that it hurt
Celso's eyes seem lost in the past
But no matter how much pain
she caused me, I went back for more
And rather than see me suffer so much
she left me and became the moon

At night I watch her, cold and remote
I tremble a little
but the suffering is gone
So saying, Celso laughs loudly
If you believe what I have just said
You are a bigger fool than I am

The First Ever Picked by Eve

For the love of a good woman
I would sever this hand
Celso says extending his crippled hand
True, it has been worthless to me
these many years, as scraggly
as a pine growing at the edge
of a windy cliff
And often it has received
the unkindly stares of strangers
Has been an object of contempt and ridicule

Even my closest friends have cringed
at its touch as if it were a crab's pincer
Nevertheless I call it the better part of me
superior to my wit in its deceitfulness
for it is the part of me most looked upon
but the least understood

Here, friends, is a flower
Crooked, I agree, and repulsive
yet it has its attraction
What would you say if I were to tell you
that the most beautiful women you know
have begged me to rest this mangled thing
upon their breasts

They think it will give them fertility
Bless them like the hand of God
Yes, this hand most wondrous to behold
like the most rare flower in Eden
The first ever picked by Eve
Yes, this hand I would cut
for the love of a good woman

Qué Pendejos Son Los Hombres Viejos

Like a drunken Chinese poet
of a thousand years ago
Celso was in love
with the moon's
reflection in the river

He had tried to embrace
the moon's reflection
like an old Chinese poet
jumping in the Yellow River
Qué pendejos son los hombres viejos

Celso had wanted to die
for an imagined love
but the river he had jumped in
was too shallow for anyone
but a poet to drown

The Poison of Her Kiss

As I am now
you will one day be
those were her
exact words, Celso said
half dressed and trembling

Aurora had brought
him a blanket
It was not
the cold of November
that made him shiver
But something
that had touched
his bones
with icy fingers

Cornelio put more wood
in the fireplace
Aurora closed the door
to the children's bedroom

Do you want some hot milk
Aurora said soothingly
as if she were talking
to one of her children

Can't you see
the poor man
needs something stronger
Cornelio interposed
And from the cupboard
he removed
a bottle of wine

All three sat

at the kitchen table
Celso still shivered
though he had wrapped
himself in the blanket
The room was warm
with a cheery glow

Now, tell us Celso
Cornelio said
in a brotherly tone
What is it
that brought you
to our house
in the middle
of the night
half dressed

Did you say
a woman
had frightened you

Aurora found it impossible
to keep back a smile

Not really a woman
Celso said
as he held tightly
to the blanket
My eyes were deceived
when I met her at the bar

Immediately
my heart became hers
I had never seen
a more beautiful woman

I should have been suspicious
Why would someone so beautiful
want someone like me
But when she began to flirt
my eyes clouded over
You know
what a beggar
my poor heart is
always running after
any crumb of affection

Celso emptied
his glass of wine
Cornelio quickly refilled it
Aurora was uncertain
if she should stay
or retire to the bedroom
But she stayed
and even poured
herself some wine

You were saying, Celso
Cornelio said
taking a sip of his wine

We had a drink or two
and then she put a hand
on my knee

Cornelio gave Aurora
a quick glance
but she pretended
not to have seen it

You can imagine
what that did to me

Celso said
and a tremor passed
through his body

Cornelio looked at Aurora
more sternly
but her eyes were fixed
on her glass of wine
A slight blush
colored her cheeks

Well, we were soon
holding hands
and without warning
she kissed me
Celso seemed
on the verge of tears

Aurora, Cornelio
said sharply
Shouldn't you
look in on the children
Aurora was on the verge
of getting up
but then she
changed her mind

I could hear them
from here
if anything was wrong
she said as she gulped
some wine

Cornelio sighed
You were saying, Celso

Did I tell you
about her eyes
Soft brown eyes
that captivated me
In those eyes
I saw tenderness
innocence and understanding
but in an instant
they could change
into fiery
passionate eyes

Her moods flickered
like a candle flame
Now passionate
then innocent
and back again
When she kissed me
my lips felt
as if they
had touched
the burning tips
of branding irons

But mixed with the pain
was a pleasure
more intense
than I had ever known

Celso got up quickly
and spit into
the dwindling fire
Cornelio threw in
another log
as Celso sat down

The poison of her kiss
will stay with me forever
I took her to my house
and we made love

Aurora, whose eyes
had been downcast
all the while
bit her lower lip
and wished that
she hadn't stayed

Her body was perfect
and I had never been
more satisfied
with any woman
Cornelio gave Aurora
a grave look
but her eyes
were still focused
on her glass of wine

I rolled to my side
and thanked God
for making me
the happiest man
in the world
and then I turned
to her and what I saw
will follow me
to my grave

Cornelio reached
for Aurora's hand

I had been making love

to a skeleton
Celso clutched tightly
to his blanket

Aurora spilled her wine
Dios mío, she said
as she made
the sign of the cross

You can't be serious
Celso, Cornelio said
in an agitated tone
as he scraped back
his chair a little

Celso began weeping

I jumped out of bed
grabbed my pants
and ran out of the house
Yours was the first light
I saw, Celso shuddered
and the tears
poured freely

Aurora and Cornelio
looked into each other's eyes
and then embraced

The loneliness
that had dogged them
throughout their lives
suddenly vanishing
as they shared
Celso's tears

THE GOSPEL ACCORDING TO CELSO (IV)

The Gospel According to Celso

In the beginning
there was a glass of wine
new and shimmering
in the sunlight
Celso tasted it
and declared it
to be good

That is how
I became a drunkard
The rotten pillar
of my community
A good for nothing
explains Celso

And Celso has preached
the message
of his special gospel
all these years
more in action and deed
than in word

Come gather around me
says Celso
carrying a jug of wine
And I will teach
you the meaning
of happiness on earth

And so it has been
Celso's divine mission
to convert people
To fill them
with the Gospel of Wine
And make them drunk
with his brand of religion

The Sermon of the Grape

Listen to Celso
preaching his gospel
The gospel of the Holy Grape

Drink of the blood
which is His blood
says Celso
holding a bottle
of red wine above his head

People pass by him
and they laugh at him
They know that he is not
to be taken seriously

Celso takes a long drink
of the red wine
and then wipes his mouth
with the back of his bare
dusty arm

Celso has many disciples
The poor, the wretched
the misfits and outcasts
of Agua Negra
They gather about him
as long as the wine holds out

A rich man will not
get through the eye of a camel
if he does not give away
his riches, Celso says drunkenly
And he passes around
the bottle of wine

until it is emptied

As soon as the wine is gone
Celso is left alone
He falls asleep
on the steps of the church
knowing that in the morning
someone will give him
the price of a bottle of wine
to make him go away

No Bed as Cold

There is no bed as cold
as the one in which a drunk sleeps
Celso says as he shares
a bottle of wine
with a friend

What woman wants to go to bed
with a drunk
Celso's friend agrees
as he watches Celso
tilt the bottle
and take a long drink

A drunk's head is filled
with rivers of wine
which drown any sparks of desire
Celso says with a sigh
carefully measuring the wine left
to the hours left in the night

His Hunger Forgotten

Every time Celso gets drunk
he says and does things
no one understands

For instance
there was the time
he was drunk
in an alley behind a bar
without a penny to his name
and it had been over a day
since he had eaten

Celso staggered
out of the alley
and nearly bumped
into two lovers
who were kissing
by the entrance
to the bar

Out of impulse
Celso took off his shirt
and began chewing it

The couple stopped kissing
and stared at him
in disbelief

This is the bread of our Lord
Celso said in a garbled voice

The woman laughed nervously
and the man growled at Celso
as they both disappeared

into the bar

Celso put on his ragged shirt
and chuckled softly
His hunger forgotten
for the time being

Devil-May-Care

Celso fell asleep drunk one night
along the Agua Negra river
The black water coursed
through Celso's sleep

It was not a quiet peace
of deep and dark waters
that the river brought
but the disquietude
of a narrow
and shallow channel
glutted with rocks

When Celso woke up in the morning
he went to wash his face
in the river
But what he saw there
so horrified him
that he got on his feet and fled

Celso ran the mile to town
nonstop and breathlessly
stormed into the church
where he had not been in years

A service was being held
But the priest stopped
with the host in his hands
inches from a young girl's mouth

Everyone turned around
to see what
the priest was staring at
Everyone gasped and the priest
dropped the chalice

without anyone seeming to notice

People were afraid to say
what it was they saw
Celso, the joker, had this time
gone too far
dressing up like the devil
with horns and tail
and a fiery red goatee

After the initial shock
people began fuming
with indignation

And the priest
Regaining his composure
Screamed at the top of his lungs

How dare you blaspheme
the house of the Lord

Death to Celso
cried a little old woman
who had often seen Celso drunk
when she walked to church

Death to Celso
and his cohort the devil
a tired-looking man shouted

He had never seen Celso work
while he labored
day and night
to keep his family
fed and clothed

Please, Celso pleaded
to the congregation
of Agua Negra
This is not a joke, see

Celso tugged at his horns
but they did not budge
He pulled at his pointed tail
but it remained stuck to him

Finally Celso grabbed his beard
and gave it such a vicious pull
that he yelled in pain
But still the beard remained
on his chin

El diablo, el diablo
everyone screamed
And as they ran in panic
to get out the back door
They overturned benches

The plaster statues
of the saints were toppled
from their lofty pillars

They crashed on the floor
breaking into thousands
of pieces

In a matter of minutes
the church was empty
Except for Celso

Looking pitiful
and with tearful eyes

Celso was such an incongruous sight
The devil on his knees
praying in the house
of the Lord

Forgive me, God
for I have sinned
Celso lamented
And his tail wagged
as he cried

The priest had warned me
many times
that I was going
to the devil
but I didn't listen

Celso covered his eyes
and wept

Abandoned by God and mankind
Celso stood up
and walked out
of the empty church

As he opened the thick
wooden doors
He saw all the people
of Agua Negra
waiting for him

Celso's heavy heart
suddenly felt
like a white cloud
in a blue day

I am not alone, he cried
and beamed at the people
as he descended the stairs

His eyes were filled
with joyous tears
and it was too late
when he noticed
that everyone
had a handful of stones

Celso was chased out of town
Stones flying all about him
like horse flies
until finally a rock
hit him on the head

Celso collapsed
Everything went dark
Black and flowing

Celso woke up
for the second time
Actually he had not woken up
the first time
It had all been a dream

Celso quickly felt his head
and not finding any horns
he quickly felt his behind
Not finding a tail there
he quickly felt his chin

Feeling a slight growth of hair
Celso nearly fainted
But then he remembered

that he hadn't shaved
in several days

Celso got on his knees
and tried to pray
But he couldn't remember
any prayers

He remembered there
was a church service
in town every morning
So he headed into town

But to get to the church
Celso had to pass by a bar
That bar always seemed
to be open no matter
what hour or day

Celso licked his lips
He tried to remember
where it was
that he was going

Oh, yes, to church
Maybe I'm being too brash
he murmured
Already he had forgotten
his nightmare

Celso entered the bar
and sat at a small table
The owner of the bar
went over to see
what Celso would have

A glass of white wine
to raise the spirits
of a fallen angel
Celso said with a smile

As the owner of the bar
walked to the counter
He yelled back

Celso, I've been thinking
of changing the name
of the bar
What do you think
of The Devil's Den

The bar owner heard
a chair overturn
When he looked back
he caught a glimpse of Celso
running out the door

He looked out the window
and saw Celso running
in a beeline towards the church

Where could Celso be going
in such a hurry
he wondered
Certainly not to church

Visitors

One night some friends
were visiting Celso
In the middle of saying something
he began crying
like a coyote

His friends stared at him surprised
When Celso finally stopped
they asked him to do it again
No, Celso said
they're gone, they're gone

The Endless Miles of Pine

Celso staggers to the door
stumbling over his cohorts
who haved passed out drunk
after an all night of drinking

When Celso opens the door
he realizes that it is
his own house he is leaving

He brushes the thought aside
and staggers in the direction
of the east where the sun
is already rising
above the mountains
The endless miles of pine

A LOST SOUL (V)

A Lost Soul

Celso had long heard stories
of balls of fire
seen at night
shooting over the mountains
or rolling on the ground

Witches, the older people had told him
You can be assured they are witches

When Celso actually saw
a ball of fire
It was not an unexpected sight

As usual, he had stayed out late
drinking wine with a friend
As Celso would tell others later
My eyes filled with tears
and I seemed to drift into a trance

That ball of fire
was swooping through the trees
like an enlarged moon
But how could that be

The ball of fire drew near
And I saw through my trance
its fur and claws
yet its body burning

I yelled for help
but nothing came out of my mouth

Everyone loved to hear
the part of the story

where the ball of fire
called Celso by his name

And how the ball of fire
led him to a cemetery
where it sank into a grave
but not before explaining
that it had once been a man

But now it was a lost soul
condemned to wander
between two worlds
and would Celso pray for him

When Witches Come Visiting

Hilarita, do you know
that there are witches about
and that these witches
would love nothing better
than to have a boiling pot
of Celso soup for dinner
and to feed my bones
to the Devil's dogs

Last Friday I heard a knock
at my door late at night
Who could it be I wondered
and got out of bed
groping for the light switch

The knocking became more emphatic
as if someone were trying
desperately to get in
Oh, my God, I thought
someone is being attacked

Unable to find the light switch
I stumbled and bumped
my way to the door
But just as I was about
to pull open the latch
I realized that I was defenseless
If there were a murderer outside
he would kill me too

My whole body trembled
in terror
My poor heart cringed
at the thought of a knife

striking suddenly
out of the dark

So I faltered and did not
open the door
but instead called out
Who is it
Even though whoever was knocking
might die at any second

In the name of God
I called again, Who is it

Then the knocking stopped
and I heard footsteps
and my blood grew colder
than the high mountain streams
flowing out of the snow

My hand was frigid
stuck to the latch
My heart started bouncing
around in my head and ears

That next morning I found
strange tracks outside my door
like those of dogs
but much larger
and they looked as if they
had been standing upright

The wooden door
had many scratches
and splinters had fallen off
I tell you Hilarita
it is a frightening thing
when witches come visiting

The Lengthening Shadows of Evening

Celso was standing
in the evening
beneath a huge crucifix
It cast a strange shadow
somewhat human
but oddly proportioned
and immense as an elephant

Celso was contemplating
the dark shadows of evening
when a skeleton stepped
out of the shadows
of the church
and walked across the plaza
in his direction

Buenas tardes
the skeleton said
when he was just
a few steps away from Celso

The shadow of the cross
covered him

Buenas tardes, Celso replied
and then asked
Are you from the cemetery

Yes, that is where I live
the skeleton answered
But quickly he added
I mean, that is where
I am dead

The shadows of evening

were lengthening
and seeing that Celso
did not have anything to say
the skeleton asked

Where do you live
if in truth you are alive
and not a skeleton like me

Oh, you can be assured
that I am alive
Celso responded
a little arrogantly

See, this is skin and flesh
covering my bones
And through my body
course many small streams
of warm blood

Celso unconsciously
felt himself
making sure
that he was not
like the skeleton

I live many miles from here
Celso added as an afterthought

May I inquire as to
your business here
the skeleton asked

I was passing by
Celso replied
And I was struck

by the shadows of this cross

In fact, all the shadows here
are very unusual
The houses, the mountains
the trees, the church

I feel that there
is something here
that I can't quite see
but that is significant

You are not the first
to stop off here
and admire our shadows
the skeleton said pridefully

We cultivate them
We grow them like flowers
When I say we
of course I mean the dead

This is our garden of shadows
They are night flowers
only opening
after the sun has set

See that shadow over there
We call it a rose
See how enveloping it is
How sensuous
A black velvety rose

While the skeleton
was distracted
pointing out the shadows

Celso quietly walked away

At the edge of town
he turned around and yelled

You are dead and I am alive
And quickly he disappeared
in a cloud of dust
as if he were
in a footrace with Death

The Dead Have No Eyes with Which to Cry

Celso was sitting
in the plaza
one late afternoon
admiring the beauty
of the blossoming trees
when a skeleton
who was passing by
stopped and asked Celso
what he was looking at

Too frightened to move
Celso nevertheless
managed to say a few words
between chattering teeth
It is spring, he stammered
and the trees are in bloom

The skeleton looked sadly
at the skeletal arms
of the trees
which were growing fuller
and would soon be obscured
as if by a covering
of skin and flesh

Ah, the skeleton sighed
if only we skeletons
were so fortunate
as to blossom anew each spring

Conquering a little of his fear
Celso managed to ask
Is it lonely being dead

Sitting down next to Celso

the skeleton answered

The beauty of these
blossoming trees
had escaped my notice
And in truth, I cannot see
the blossoming trees
but through your eyes

Are you blind
Celso asked
innocently

I have no eyes
how would I see
the skeleton replied
with sarcasm

But don't you see me
Celso asked
finally managing
to sound calm
You must have seen me
when you stopped to talk

It is a strange thing
to explain
the skeleton said
as his bony knee brushed
Celso's trembling leg

I cannot see anything living
except through the eyes
of the living
When I look at you
I am in fact seeing myself

May I please use your eyes
to weep a little
Everything is so beautiful

Not seeing that he had
much choice in the matter
Celso nodded his head
Besides, he was so frightened
that tears would be
a welcome relief

The tears began to pour
out of Celso's eyes
And in no time
his shirt was drenched

Forgive me, the skeleton sobbed
It has been so long
since I had a good cry

While the skeleton
was rubbing
his empty eye sockets
Celso got up
and began walking away
first slow then faster

Come back
the skeleton yelled
Bring back my eyes

Celso was now running
The tears pouring
down his cheeks

For many days after

Celso's eyes were tearful
And when people
asked him
what was the matter
He would answer quizzically
that the dead
have no eyes
with which to cry

Celso Talking to the Moon

I am afraid sometimes
Celso says
as he licks the wine
off his lips

I am afraid of the blood
sweeping across my body
Celso takes a swig of wine

The problem is
that I fear life
as much as I fear death
Celso shivers even though
it is a warm night

You are lucky
You are a woman
Celso gazes longingly
at the moon

When you are afraid, you cry
Tears come easily to you

Celso takes a long drink
trying to get his heart so drunk
that it will let go
of a few miserable tears

BREATH OF FLOWERS (VI)

Breath of Flowers

It was raining and the sun was shining
A wolf must be giving birth
or an idiot is paying his debt
Celso thought

And before crossing the bridge
he took two steps backwards
like he had seen the farmers do
before crossing an irrigation ditch

Across the river lived his neighbors
There was an odor of flowers in the house
yet there wasn't a flower to be seen

Where did you get the flowers
Celso asked Esmeralda
I haven't smelled one in months
Isn't it too early for flowers

Esmeralda winced at these words
and her body bent like a wilting flower

Are you all right, Celso said
watching Esmeralda hold precariously
to the kitchen table

Esmeralda straightened slowly
and gazed at the sun through the window

How curious, Celso smells them too
she mumbled to her husband
who was sitting across the table

Tell me Celso, do you smell lilacs
That is what Arcenio smells

But I smell wild roses

Arcenio looked at Celso with a worried gaze
and spoke in a trembling voice

Esmeralda has a good imagination
It has spread to her nose
I try to humor her

Celso could not think of a word to say
There was that breath of flowers
so distinct, it was as if he were
in the middle of a garden

How stupid I am, Celso thought
suddenly realizing what he smelled

It was in Esmeralda's face
which so resembled a collapsing rose
in her body which was faltering
In her eyelids which were like two
colorless petals

Unable to apologize or leave
Celso looked out the window
to see what Esmeralda was gazing at
A rainbow spanned the river
and the sky was turning red

A Widow's Dance

One night as Celso
stumbled home drunk
he noticed that the mountains
seemed to be dancing
but it was a slow
patient dance
done by black veiled widows
A dance to make
the heart turn cold

He crossed his heart
and said Blessed is the Virgin
and so is her Child
So saying he felt
greatly relieved
But he couldn't escape
the strange feeling
that the mountains
were in procession
to a funeral

For who, for who
Celso thought frantically
If someone could have touched
Celso's heart at that moment
he would have felt
something so cold
that it would have burned

As He Shuts the Door behind Him

Celso dreads old age

The children will throw
rocks at me
and the dogs will
nip at my heels
he says to no one in particular

Celso downs a glass of wine
and grimaces

There was a time
it was a pleasure to drink
he says as he pours
another glass of wine

But any more it has become a job

Celso dutifully empties
that glass of wine
and staggers to the door
of the bar

I have seen children
spit in their parents' eye

In the wind I can spit
in my own eye
Celso says as he shuts
the door behind him

Newlyweds

What a life I've lived
Celso sighs
as he sits down at a table
where a newly wed couple
is gazing into each other's eyes

All the good women I have let
slip through these hands
Celso says sadly
as he looks around for a waitress
The newlyweds are oblivious
to Celso's presence

If I could live this life over
Celso says with a nervous laugh
I would settle down early
with the first woman
who looked at me
with love-filled eyes

The waitress comes over
Celso gazes into her eyes
but finding no love there for him
he orders a glass of wine
The waitress walks away
shaking her head

It frightens me when I think
of all the nights I've wasted
Celso sighs again

The newlyweds have not heard
a word Celso has said
and with their eyes
they continue the lovemaking
of the night before

Celso's Rejuvenation

It came as quite a shock to me
says Celso, to wake up one morning
and find out that the young women
were no longer giving me the eye
Undoubtedly it had been years
since a young woman had looked at me
and felt the blush of lust
rise to her face

I looked around and noticed
that the only women who bothered
to say more than hello and good-bye
were the viejitas
The little old women of the town
who I always thought of as
so and so's grandmother and such

It was then that I decided
to take a good hard look
at myself in the mirror
and much to my dismay
I discovered that I was a viejito

I had always considered myself
to be quite a lady's man
despite the fact that I had
been turned down by more women
than any other man in history
There were enough who said yes
to more than make up

I had always loved women more
than I have loved my own self
And there is no woman

no matter how ugly
who I would not lay down
my life for

And so without as much
as a good-bye kiss
I found myself dismissed
from the hearts and affections
of those I loved
The firm feel of their breasts
and the chapels of their thighs
where I paid my devotionals
would now be locked to me
by that cruel jailer, old age

At first I was tempted to get drunk
as I did so often in my youth
and I even went out
and bought me a bottle of wine
But my hands trembled so
that I could not bring
the bottle to my lips

I am truly doomed I thought
I have grown so old that
I cannot even get drunk
After having many unpleasant thoughts
and thinking of myself
as being all but dead and buried
I was revived by a spark, a thought
that had me dashing out of the house
on sturdy legs that a minute before
I wouldn't have thought
capable of movement

And there true to her routine

was the widow Doña Carmela
coming down the steps
of the venerable old church
Proud and erect and with a missal
in one hand and her purse in the other
she walked slowly in my direction
I waited until she was
directly in front of me
and then I collapsed

I feigned death and she got
on her knees before me
as she had done in the church
minutes earlier
Doña Carmela had been a nurse
until she had retired
so I figured she knew
how to revive me
I kept my eyes closed
anxiously awaiting her mouth

But no, nothing came
No wet lips
No vigorous pumping of my chest
with her legs astride me
Did I play my part too well, I thought
Does she take me to be truly dead

The suspense was too great
and I opened one of my eyelids
just the tiniest bit

Aha, just as I thought
said Doña Carmela
quickly getting up from the street
where she had been kneeling by my side

I see the stories I have heard
about you are true, she said
towering above me with the sun
behind her head emitting a halo

I quickly lifted myself off my back
and prostrated myself before her feet
Do you have no shame, Doña Carmela
said sounding very vexed
There are people who will see us
For heaven's sake, act your age
It was then that I looked up
at her with a look
of adoration in my eyes

Forgive me Doña Carmela, I pleaded
getting up on my knees
I must have passed out from the heat
and when I opened my eyes and saw you
with the sun's rays around your hair
like a halo, why I thought
that I had died
and that you were the Virgin Mary

Doña Carmela was taken aback
by what I told her
and she reached down for me
and picked me up and embraced me
Poor unfortunate man, she cried
And here I thought you had
been trying to deceive me

She held me tenderly and wept softly
And arm in arm we walked
towards her house
Her missal somewhere lost and unmissed

Old age is not so bad I thought
thinking of my youth
and the many times I went to bed alone

Celso's Story about China

I know next to nothing about China
except that it is a very old country
And there is a story that I once heard
about a Chinese poet who fell in love
with a water spirit

He spent his life by the river
just so he could catch a glimpse of her
every other day or so
and that was enough of love for him
and he probably would have been
very content if that had continued
until his death

But when he was a very old man
she ceased to be illusive
and appeared to him fully
Of course she was nude and very beautiful

It had been so long
since the poor poet had known a woman
that he did not know what was expected of him
And all that he could do was grin
Needless to say, the river spirit
was very disappointed and wept bitterly

All her life she had waited for this moment
but she had been too timid
And now she had this leering
simpleton of an old man
who could do nothing but grin

Ashamedly she dove back into the river
and the poet was never

to catch a glimpse of her again

That is a very sad story
says Celso's friend
It reminds me of my old age
I feel like weeping
over the lost flesh
The voluptuous curves
I will never feel again

Celso nods in agreement
I do not know that country or its people
but I cry when I think of all the people there
Of all the loves begun and ended
Of all the flesh touched and lost

I weep for all those who held
happiness in their hands
and yet did not know what to do with it

Celso's Detractors

When are you
going to die
everybody asks me
Celso says
with a grin

I've already
outlived my detractors
Those who said
I was headed
for an early grave

Celso grins
His natural teeth
glistening
for all to see

And yet I live on
And those who were
so careful
and always made plans

Well, not even
their children
visit their graves
anymore

Winter in His Bones

Celso claims that there is
a winter chill in his bones

I am between ninety
and a hundred years old, he says
And the spring won't
thaw out my bones anymore

Celso still gets up early
to make a fire in his woodstove
He rises before the sun
like his ancestors before him

I spend more time
by the stove, he says
Sometimes I feel a chill in me
that could make the pine trees shiver

When I'm dead, Celso says
Tie my jaws together with wire
There are times my teeth chatter so
I think they will never stop

The Other Side of the Horizon

I am Celso, scared and annoyed
at my stupidity
I thought age would cure it
When I was a child
I wanted to grow older
Be independent, in control
For all the many years that have passed
I have gone no great distance
from that child

How many years have passed
and I have traveled like a snail
from that child
I dreamed of great things
over the mountains
over the horizon of the plains
Every mountain I have crossed
has been a disappointment
and I have never been
to the other side of the horizon

Old age has gotten you nowhere, Celso
I tell myself
Nowhere but in trouble
I find myself thinking
more about death
and I am filled with fears
But then that too
is bound to be a disappointment
nothing like what the child
would have imagined it to be